NORTHUME
POEMS

BY SIMON OVERTON

FOR FIONA

AFTER SUCH KNOWLEDGE, WHAT FORGIVENESS?
-T.S. ELIOT

ISBN 978-1-4452-3260-7

SIMONOVERTON@ME.COM

Northumbrian Poems

By Simon Overton

Riding the Bounds

Above all, we must keep firmly in mind what it
means to be a human being. Kierkegaard

(I)

The call of geese in the thrush throated woods
And dappled writhing wings, the water's waist
Is bruised by feet, throats fumbling for fish.
Heaven's intermediaries, wild they course
Silver streams, slime; pursuivant to God's ghost,
Heralds to spring sun, the slush of fierce frost.
Necks jib and feathers fan the forceful rite
Of calling. Their dark eyes reflect a young boy
His knuckles raised and knees grained from kneeling;
Squatted on gravel. The rasp of shingle
And the pitting of a bird by cruel hands
Cuthbert stands up and walks towards Melrose
Across the estates, heather and hogweed,
Striding measured moors of pheasant and snipe.
A prayer of palms on thorns his feet suck mud,
The schooling of silence governs the tongue
And blesses bruises, the slight of thistles.
Five miles before behind, footsore a boy
Returns to his land with the still warm eggs
To a people who have seen the raided light
Reave into darkness and evening's shadows.
Then traffic is hurrying across the Tweed
And bonds are electric, griping the mind
With blood which has clotted the fiscal soil
And turned the bounds to inward pastures.

Night opens through the folds of a bird's wing,
Supine the nape of a twisting neck scoops

The gravel in a curve of acknowledgement;
The circumference of love is the boundary
Of God, the clumsy reckonings, the haste
To unspeak language and recall the beloved.
Refolding wings merely languors hours;
The word once spoken moves out of time
As salmon slipped from the weir's palm
Dash into the brilliant darkness of light.

The long road descends to the peopled bay
And herling gild the waves where the gulls scud,
From this hill the soil is slit by the Tweed
And the silt of memories gathers in her mouth,
The immaculate dawn above the waters
Buries the mountains with a feint of embrace.
Light needles the retina with sharp rays,
The refractive warmth of a yellowed stamen;
Here Cuthbert first failed and met himself:
The soul, the heart, the thing, the flaming forth
The bright self immersed in the spark of God.
To disect and measure the optic nerve
Could never retrieve that heraldic light,
Nor could a knowledge of neurons divulge
The moment of meeting to the calloused brain.
All things flame each other with the fragrance
Of God, the splendid moment as beings pass.

(II)

The smell of oak-smoke, salmon baked breakfast
Risen up with curses for prayers, he bathes
In the blessing of water, balm of ice,
The hymn of the winds in his chattering teeth,
Somehow changed and awake he greets the sun,
Casting his coracle on the grey current

To go hauling nets through uncertain depths
In a long parabola against the shore.
The movement of being in a flush of sweat
As sated sinews compress in motion
And rhythmically stress the power of bone,
As hands buckle waters and tug at nets,
Review their absence, then trudging the shore
He moves again through the fluid sand.
Oars harden palms and callous blisters, back
Bruises chafe in the transcendent heat
And again he is steering the strong wave
Of hidden salmon, who courting his boat
Conjure their scales from his coarse grasp as he
Remains adrift on the furrowed shore.

Charcoal has taste, and the crunch of fillet
Belies the flesh sweetened reel of bone
The disguarded organs observed and burnt
Stink and indulge the visceral senses
Perverse that this liver gave the creature life
Or this spleen lay the creature's spirit low
Odd that these things are not the thing itself
But rather some ghostly brother labours
A winder of feeling to clockwork fins
Polisher up of these bright shiny scales
And jeweller to blank, now pustular eyes-
One has burst, does that cousin thus take wing
Or has he always lurked, an alterego
To his friend, himself, the fish, the thing.
How well he struggled, muscular in the nets
Until he reclined on the baking sand
Out of his medium in the drowning air
Flailing against the extraction of death
Towards ancient remembrances of light.
How often have we swum within our God

And found the medium strange, the foam
Expansive and the current obscure,
The shore a telescopic absurdity.
In drowning we aquaint ourselves
With the sway of water, the subtle mark,
The thumbprint of God on our fledgling form.
So Cuthbert thought as he stretched his hands
And washed their blood in the amniotic waves.

(III)

An abbey of wattle, of mead, matins
And silent cloisters; birdsong in the throat
Refines quinquagesima with psalms. The smoke
Of censors plummets up with abandon
Wafting the prayers of saints to the rafters
Or anointing the soles. Salutaris Hostia,
And other mumblings woven in gold, thread
Stirred in oil, thin chords, the cacophony
Of an opaque air refracting the ethereal.
Beyond the screen is the sound of God
And chasubles daubed with griffins and birds
An impressionist smear of cobalt and green.
Here a bickering and bone-picking people
Abstains from holiness. The churches chatter
Only quenched in a moment of uplifted
Bread; God incognito amongst the yeast.
Outside, the host of the sun is raised
And smelts the fields in its core of love.
Christ resurrected to a fiscal world,
Christ in the sawing of wood and the harvest,
Christ in the saying of words and the silence,
Christ in the turning of waves and the soil,
His geese resplendent in the warming rays.
Would that all the Lord's people were prophets

That shoulder bones should sprout as wings, awkward
Except in the sleek ascent, odd protrusions
From a body politic; seraphic weights.
What a work is a man, his form of flesh
An imperfect tissue about the bone
The apprehensive murmur of the heart
A paragon of form, the fragile brain
Admirable in the expression of vapouress
Thoughts, a quintessent clown, and yet to me
Magnificent in the failure of his faculties.

(iv)

Then he came, the Lord, the giver of life,
Arrogant and haughty, his fluttering arms
Epileptic and flailed on the cobble stones
His mouth a babble of foreign words.
Let there be requiems sung for the soul
And let the light fall unrefracted by
Stained glass and shards of comprehension.
Do away with wreaths of corn and daisies
Let the faithful stand with bleeding gums
And mark his passing with their certainty.
Let laughter choke the gaping tears, and may
The earth retch his diseased corpse. Into
Light he may come, omnipresent and vital,
The thrush may lay her fragile eggs, and nurse
The speckled young, her disgruntled genes.
He shall see it as it is, amongst the hedgerows,
The brooks alive with the fervour of thought
And the fat-headed crocus shall spurt its blooms
To mark the memory of his going by.
The oak arced by lighting shall curse his god
And damp thunder trespass on sterile ground,
But he shall have no gods; being so caught up

In the milieu of movement he shall dance
And not pray; unaware of the medium.
He will crouch with Cuthbert in the warm cell
Refracted on the walls through narrative
Flames; he who was woven from earth and stars.
The Fathers were right, so Cuthbert thought,
Stooping down to draw water, a saint must doubt
The feet which have trespassed amongst the rocks;
These gods imprisoned in paper lanterns.
For he appeared in the upper room amongst
Them, when the doors were locked and windows barred,
He appeared and Thomas dared not touch him;
The chivalrous flower struggling to burst
Beyond the weak wafer of the bodies husk.
Let us recall that puissance, thought Cuthbert,
(The bucket's rope chafing his frozen hands.)
To embrace the swell with impervious grasp
Requires one, delicate, for liquid cupped
Exploits the cracks between fingers and thumb.

The axe slopped into the tender sap, green
Moss encaustic on the broken bark signals
The dampness of the season, where leaves rot
The splintered wood is left, white and human.
For he is cutting kindling, a kind of prayer
To the creature, our lady, in the dead tree.
Arthritic her aching fists clutch, and feet
Shuffle in the gnarled knots of cerebral earth.
Far by the lake a cob's wax wings, wrestle
Their medium between swimming and flight.
The voracious beak strains, pouts and pounds
The mathematics of music with a mad sound,
Their necks taut, drinking the sun and their
Wing beat stirring the urgent dawn. They
Have risen from the water, the weed and slime,

Retracing their course to thrush throated woods.

Lindisfarne

When we sat in the ruins of Cuthbert's cell
The tide turned like my hand across your breast,
Returning through earth's resurgent memories
To encircle a moment of Eucharist
With a murmuring wind, whilst lost in us
I faltered on the threshold of my thoughts,
Desiring your body and the touch of earth,
Fire for the darkness between heavens.
A sacrament, as embraced we were poured
Inviolable with the force of foam and surf.

We are shards reflecting one vast mirror
Till that mirror evanescent in the fierce sun,
Melts into the depths as rain to water
Mercurial in the arteries of the dark earth
The human tenderness of your arms
Enfolding my body into your soul,
From the myriad knots of root and vein
To the thundering swell of resurgent calm,
The transcendent murmur from this shoal
Of you and I caught in communion.

Bowed under the wave of each other we
Were swimmers in a rainbow's myriad hues,
A choir from a single voice, the noise
Of covenant that Cuthbert never knew.
Whose ruined face with agony looked in
Upon the flood, the Eucharistic tide.
Wind rattled timbers, desiring the blaze
Of a kindred spirit to lodge with him,
Yet ashore on shingle I stepped aside
From yourself kneeling into the waves.

Ic becom eowr man

Come Holy Spirit from the four winds come,
To a city thirsting enough for rain,
Be incarnate and turn to press in time
Your face in the water's unshaken veins.
As salmon kicking at the poacher's line
Our minds are yielded in the churning stream,
Whilst to hang like a falcon high above
And look on the scaffolded Nazarene

Is beyond what our being can withstand,
Our God is smaller than our heart may know.
Civilisations fall and the soul commends
One quiet miracle to overthrow
Everything, in a soft consuming wind,
The town shimmering under Halidon hill
And the River Tweed lapping against the sea.

We have human faces but eagle's wings
To plummet our hearts in eternity,
In the arid heat of indifferent soils
And the ditches and mires of history.
We are husks of the moments anointing
When the earth is sweet with cornflowers and sun
In the hollow caverns of the city,
Breathe into us both my comforter, come.

Duns Law

Wind-song amongst the trees and the flowers
Of the dead uncurl their faces, the squat
   Hill fashioned by tramplings of time
   And Standards raised above the peat.
      Drum clouds; Duns Law is still
And shuttles weave voices through sodden strands.
Cauterised by cannon a thousand blades
Of grass are bled in the cordite breeze
And the thin brotherhoods of death embrace
   The rag and bone of urgent soil.

Fumbling of arms, an exchange of kisses
And thorns like words sharpen into the throat
   With vowels for wives and husbands
   And consonants pledged, a sad shout
      Through streets, and on the hill.
The ancestral voices beat in the ears
And the tatters of banners pinion nerves,
Dissecting the articles of a man
With the silent government of the earth,
   And ledgers less sacramental.

Yet dawn has not poured across our nations,
Blood sky awaking to uncurl the arms
   Of those barricaded by blankets
   To the nervous summons of bird songs.
      To an army dispersed,
With love and laughter in the dancing trees
And a Credo of summer on the mouths
Of those who pummeled their wives in fear
Or listen on, taught under ancient clouds
   To love and suffering unrehearsed.

The Working Class

No kings are buried under Halidon Hill
And the mingled dead have soaked through the soil,
The combine's drone awakes mere insects,
And clouds of chaff where no others toil.

History is simply the recounting of debts,
The old firm divisions above the Tweed,
Ancient politic for new agendas
Of which the dead being dead have no need.

My brotherhood of earth, eternal youth,
What heads gashed crimson to stand upon you,
What drums rattled to farcical masters
And whispered on till the grass regrew?

We, as the moment's essential labourers
Have tarried enough under government deeds
And drafted another turn of the soil
With a misheard word of bureaucratic need.

You my companions, are you all dying?
Martyrs who confess yet recant their pleas?
Who is this victor that feeds on you? You
Bitter at the dictates of their history.

Gloria

Ikon I

Glory to God for the fruits of the earth
And the landscape curving like your shoulders,
For this Mass of the World teeming with birth,
The crust of the soil broken with flowers.
Glory for the mountains embraced with snow
Where our bodies have left their faint impress
Of souls, haze-like caught up in the rainbow
Of memory and loss and the sun's dark bliss.
To the rivers swollen with spawn and rain
And all in the breathing of God, praise her
For all this land, this moving sheet of flame,
Morning's rays, and you and I, this holy
Summation of furrows and pools of ice
For the touch of your hands like streams, glory

Ikon II- For My Grandfather

Death overcame him this afternoon
And the white stained sheets were folded away;
A bed left vacant in a sterile room
With fresh linen where once the body lay.
Late, I did not see this sweet angry man
Insane as a child and stubborn as stone,
Nurses came and went in the stale morning
Opening the windows to his first haven,
And this man whom I loved, who hammered nails
Who whittled away wood, both sang and cursed,
Is gone, and his house and garden are still.
His wife lays the table with her lips pursed
And I did not see him before he died,
Nor felt his Presence in the hospital.

Ikon III

On Cocklawburn shore where the rocks rise
Like bulwarks in the bastion of the sea
I ran in the barley of the thick tide
And rolled the shawl of the sands around me.
Your long hair spread in the curls of the waves,
And trout were plucked out to swim in your hands
Till the Tweed was rank with the glory of God,
The fictile consonance of the land.
These tiny vowels of our brief moment
Have opened language in a blush of sound
And witnessed against the face of heaven,
The strong call of the gull above the fields
And the ransacked walls of the tumbled dunes;
Both stained with the blood of oil and diesel.

Ikon IV-Tweedmouth

Hosanna for the lank curve of the hills
And the ribs of light on the rivers back,
In the certain close of the livid day
On petty words and uncertain contracts.
They have all become a part of myself,
Of deeper richness than the last embers.
From Marygate to along New Bridge Street
And to where the harbour walls are ended;
They have all been caught in the seagull's flight
To hang in the silent wharf of memory,
Cold carrion crowding my churning thoughts
With hosannas for the pig-headed grip of the sea
And the lanterns slung from returning boats;
Hosanna, I would rhyme if the tides could echo.

Ikon V

In the bright eclipse of your tattered hair
Where thoughts like talons grapple with strangers
And wrestle God in the ploughed up earth, rage
Dying, living on the barb of a stare.
The thrush's thin eggs are bled in sunlight
And small spines ripple on the river's back,
Till as salmon struggling in shallow becks
We are choked upon our gills for contact
Less fallow than furrows, more soul than mind.
This August's shoots are furred with mould, become
Too hesitant in nature, in the forged might;
The surrender, the yellow dew and fog of autumn,
That I would tether my hands in your hair
To recharge my thoughts in that other condition.

Ikon VI

Prayer, the whispering of the soul to God,
The heartfelt murmur which without consent
Is uttered in breathing, the loved one's ear
Receptive to the silence, the lips grown tense
With a fusillade of words. The banquet
At which one is girded to serve and pass
Their hands unbidden across the shoulders.
The feast where the mouth with food is massed
Usurping senses with a deep caress
That pinions the soul as her wounded hands
Clutch cheek and jaw in a feint of rapture
Less chivalrous. The knowledge of demanding
Bread, of asking and receiving nothing,
Except arms held wide in deep dementia

Ikon VII

What use our suffering immobile Lord?
Cruel king, our love, impaling and impaled
You hold out hope that is so high I stretch
And reach the wood, but cannot touch the nails
To tear my fingers, draw tacks, claw you free
Kicking obscenely in the leaden air.
In the fog of Emmaus whose is this
Fleeting face that ponders the glass ? I stare
But yet no eyes acknowledge mine, this meal
Records a passing presence, left without
Human touch. I break bread as though to seal
Your stained face in panes beside the altar;
You pass in the night having brushed against
The poor pavane of these human events.

A Spiritual Castle

Say that you and I should fix our minds
To build a castle above the dunes,
Shore the walls with imagination
When winds pull all around to ruins.
Then we have lived beneath our shadow,
Filled the cellars with a people's tithe,
Burnt the timbers under every thought
As mortar and stone stifle our lives.

The ultimate fealty of the earth
Returned to nature, while we two love
Like gulls furrowing after the plough.
Yet thought upon thought is not enough
When heaven rushes about the walls
And oceans breach and flood the land,
The spirit faltering, ascending the stairs,
Clutching the soul with nervous hands.

Maybe God has pealed across the fields
Rung our faces in the empty mime
Of our grinding minds, the granary
Of an abstract millstone churning time.
The table laid with emptiness
As silence winnows and threshes words
For the infinite moment when God
Is fed in servitude to a servile world.

Say that birds shall eat the meat of kings
And grate their black wings against the sun,
Soar in indifferent flames of nothing
Through our instants of liberation:
We have built a spiritual castle
And walked alone along Bamburgh's coast,

Cold at the roughness of the summer,
And at a moment breached, burnt and lost.

Homage to Lydia Cholij

If saints are in need of a saint then she
Is blessed enough to be less divine,
Her bow has fiddled on the soul
The thin symphony of serenity
To death left dead behind.

She has split the night apart and shown us
Through a crack of light the celestial
Form of natural and human things,
The fall in its ultimate nonsense
Beside God's endless will.

And if heavy limbs grow thicker than ash
Then the sure yet quiet Holy Ghost,
Wafting the lights beneath the hill,
Will break in the beauty of her laugh
And make her his own host.

Canticle for St.Francis

Far from my house where the Whiteadder runs,
And scrapes its belly across the ford,
Burnishing banks with the fire of frost
As the heat of labour swiftly pours
Full fathoms of water in the Tweed's depths,
The quintessence of God carved in the tides.
Brother Wind is unwounded by the rough earth,
And Sister Earth by the gloss of his sighs.
                    Beads like mercury adorn the corn,
                        The sun is fierce
And waters pour where the spirit has gone.
Come Father, come Creator, Son of the poor,
Last dew of morning in the fields furrows,
Majestic in the rays of our bright host
                    Where the Whiteadder runs.

The valley is dressed in its summer shades
And swollen apples brown in the heat,
Held in the store of all that is and shall be;
A grain of wafer and cider sacraments,
The full fruition of an immobile Lord.
Brother trout heaves through the weir's palms
Climbing the scaffold to the spawning shales,
To the heavy desert and immortal calm
                    Of one who touched the tears of God,
                        The force of water.
Beat of spirit and wings in the darkness,
Towers and cities and lanterns swinging,
Diseased faces in the immaculate light
And the weight of God in the turning soil
                    Both beautiful and bright.

Up above a light fluorescent and fierce,

A negative of limbs weighed beneath the cross,
The stones are bright and the hillside dark,
Blanched faces jerking to revue their loss
And balance the scales of contradiction.
Brother sun most firm in the poverty
Of your giving, gorged on darkness I wake
To the glory of Merse mists and valleys.

              Rebuild my church which as you see
                  Is touched by sunlight,

And militant amongst the crocus and thorns
With the movement of laughter in the still
Wind, banks built scoured, gashed and turned
Fitful in the ebb under Halidon hill

              Where the Whiteadder runs.

22 March 1997

On Temporary Blindness

I stand at the door and wait for darkness
Staring at the nest where the sparrows died.
Only earthly lights shine across from Berwick
And the moon grins black on the clotted soil.
My vision is poor and my days of blindness
Squat painful and ugly in my passive brain.
Unseen the surgeon played out his hand,
Finite and paltry before haemorrhaging veins.
You saw my birth and my infinite dying,
The forking of memories in flaccid graves.
If I had stayed blind would I have seen you?
Lean on the joist by the open doorway
A lantern clenched in your bleeding hand, held
Useless to my face and my unhealed eyes.

On the New Service

Is this morning's Magnificat.
A clatter of tambourines and toys
And pews full of bourgeois families
Frightening Our Lady with their noise.

Is this the evangelist's liturgy;
To break a people beneath their book
And sacrifice every sacrament
For a user-friendly, modern look.

Is this then the apostolic church
Praying with Francis and other saints?
Why this shrieking and waving of arms?
Why do they not stare and contemplate?

Why do they prefer urbanus Christ
Instead of the screaming Nazarene?
Byrd knew well the agony of faith
And awoke to the blood of his dreams.

The Mirror

Our breath froze firm on the corrie walls, ice
Caked our faces, head-torches spattered sleet
On the rimed rock. In the rough corrie
Ptarmigan have fled and the hare like moon
Springs through the clouds with his amber breath.
Benighted we gaze at the days gathering,
The kneading of ourselves in a hard climb;
The shape of God in the formless spindrift.

There was divinity in the action of our hands
On rock, the apprehension of ourselves
When we fell and the violent tug back
From that wild presence, to hack snow again
With an axe or place a screw, to struggle, climb,
Master our passions and admire each crystal.

Today we crawled up above Braeriach
And saw the sun burrow through nimbus clouds
Out from the rapture of our unfertile hearts
We turned back again through restless darkness.

Thursday, 20 April 2000

The Plantation

New gods for the acropolis

The plantation is awkward below the crag
The thin wind kisses the unseen branches
Whilst tanned we sweat on the chalked rock
Muscled and gorgeous in the lank heat

Across the broken fence the spruce open

Beckoning towards apprehensive depths
They have watched our labour, admired pleasure
In their cool stillness of buried sunlight

Mallory

Sagarmatha's sugar face has wept
Ice, and her breath has scissored the clouds.
Bleached silk, she is dressed above me now
And the Chinese lantern of her moon
Hangs faint in the azure folds of sky.
A Buddha, I crouch in desiccating winds,
Torn clothing revealing alabaster flesh
And my mother weeps her stones across me.
Let me leap from the circle of my dreams
Till waxen wings melt across my elbows,
May feathers never crack, nor my body fall
Dashed on bamboo spears of frost, the brocade
Of rock like green shoots on my shoulders,
The sun stuffed into my gasping mouth.
I have called her name and my heart has heard
Her closing the blinds on an English night,
Turning aside in the dark drawing-room
And holding a picture with damp fingers.

May 99

Kairos

Before my hand knocked upon the door;
　　　　　　　　My knuckles tanned
And the breeze curling against the shore,
　　　　　　　　Pressing the land.

Before my hand knocked and fingers fell
　　　　　　　　To rap dark wood
I saw the grain, combed out like a shell,
　　　　　　　　Then I entered.

St. John Passion

Risible Humanite- Baudelaire

i) Tenebrae

Somewhere I am stumbling in the ditches
And across the bones of my comrades,
Skulls strewn like petals in the wounded earth
With the embers of civilisation.
I have lain with the living in the dust
And prayed for Jerusalem to descend;
For a host of Seraphs and rushing streams.
Hunger is gnarling within my belly
And somewhere I have entered into hell
As one would enter into nothingness,
Not with the spark of my resilience
But compliance to our indifference.

I have begun to understand my soul
Within the rhythm of my existence,
A forest that ends, only, in desert.
I have watched the geese return for summer.
And felt the mysteries of the twilight,
Of the waters glazed with a little sun
And myself and my love amongst the reeds,
I have begun to understand, nothing.
Maybe I have understood the moment;
Then, or those faces in silent hunger
Walking on the bones of their ancestors,
Their children; maybe and only maybe.

These human faces are more than Auschwitz,
Hands limp on the wire of history.
Look, he is forgotten, that Son of Man,

He is finished, left dying with the past,
These corpses resurrected from the earth
And their ashes sprinkled to the wind.
My Christ if only your angel were sent
To touch my tongue with a bead of water.
But I have only glimmers of heaven
When my soul is dissolved in ecstasy,
And I glimpse the spirit of my beloved
Only to be left in utter darkness.

This prison is the freedom of my mind,
The lethargy that finds me on the streets
Struggling against the crowd towards my love
And calling in the silence of my soul,
As these thousands drift on to Hades.
This, our life, is a pigment of nothing,
An iridescence from a fractured being,
The simple ground of a quiet desert
Where we need only one Resurrection.
Somewhere I am stumbling in the ditches.

ii) A Cine-film

There you go, standing by the field.
The thick odour of poppies in the breeze
As you and your sister skip down the lane
And clomp in a stream, clamber on a stye.
Laughing but without the sound of laughter
As you hide and play in your little house
Or tumble and roll on the heavy lawn.

There you go, talking to ghosts by the wall,
Grazing your soul on the past and reaching
Into the dim infancy of adulthood.
Nations are broken in the palm of God,

And you squat and stare in the tumid brook,
Spearing the minnows, whilst momentary words
Are memories winnowed in a rising wind.

And at Guernica the children were laid in rows,
Little bundles thrown on the wooden carts.
And I tried to venture into childhood,
Into the kingdom of your youthful face,
To swim slow against the current of time
And know the rich vintage of our being.

iii) Pastoral

When the hawthorn hedges were blanched with buds
And the voluptuary drone of harvest bees,
Showers swelled the grain and out of heaven
A rainbow, bent itself towards the soil,
Into the Cheviots and my waiting mind.
Rich with the blossom of eternity,
As if the looking glass of nature could
Resolve its beams to a silent maker,
And rivers sing in their glazed reflection.

These waters flow on across the meadow,
Past pine, sycamore and derelict farms,
Towards the whispers of an empty sea.
Fishing boats are rotting on harbour walls
And hell is the hours of degradation
In a seedtime that will not know harvest.
I may wait and wait and queue for nothing
Content with the factory in my mind
And a few smiles of less desolation.

Only, here I smell the colour of God,
The bitter incense of utter darkness,

The touch of the intangible moment
Of reconciliation beyond being,
The fruition of my Northumberland.
And Christ the Achilles heal of God
Once rattled behind like an empty tin
With sinews taught on the tree of history
Shall stand gaunt, his face towards the wind.

And you my unthinking, unspeaking God,
In the hollow heat of a summer day
I have felt the anger of your silence,
When the fire dances through foreign coals
I have lain motionless in the movement
Of my love and held her supine body
In all the fury of this spinning world,
Till my hands bleed, burn and tear at the earth,
And I have no words except child, child, child.

iv) Iesum

Dwelling on the threshold between two worlds,
The feast of darkness and incandescent light,
Children are stirring while the candles burn,
Faces touched by the breath of Icons.
Here the snow is no longer wet with blood
And the first swollen buds break the crust of earth.
Dwelling in the moment when being is weighed
Before it's momentary swing into God,
Dwelling in the sensuous hands of the dusk
As nativities bare a resurgent Christ,
Half son of earth; without bread or wafer
We stand in the vault and Eucharist of our being
And lack surrender to the quiet ghost.

Who is this knocking on the inner door,

I have entered the house and seen no-one,
Through the window the beauty and swell of
The sea, nearer still the Northumbrian hills,
And I heard your steps in a distant room.
Whose are those voices singing in the church,
Echoing in the tower till the beams crack,
Till history is the torrent in our minds
Merely lights reflected in the dark glass.
The table is empty and the walls bare,
The shutters are burnt by Pentecost.

And I have dwelt in the darkness of God
A tenant to the silent watchful host,
He who screams like a madman at the,
Final hour, bleeding and bruising for love.
In the thin golden thread of consciousness
I have felt the expanse rung like a bell
And stared out to sea from Bamburgh's dunes
Through storms for a sail or second coming
Instead of an emaciated flogged Jew.
Knowing the backwardness of our nation
I have waited and waited for nothing.

Where is our Lady of human sorrow,
The still sad face beyond the veil as we
Scramble in the mire without acceptance,
The trees are gnarled by the weight of heaven
And here is no Presence but indifferent rain.
The distant church is dull, the singing faint,
The voices of Aidan, Oswald and Bede
Caught up in the childlike tongues of flame,
The silent depths of the cauldron ocean.
The oars dug the waves as we rowed for Beal;
And the ebbing and flowing were the same.

Three Pavanes On the Death of Christ

(I)

Christus, peal bell, blow hammered word,
The opening of wings in my clenched hands,
Flesh that has form in my fingertips
And breathes in the kyrios of the land.
Unseen Presence, you linger in absence
And know the winds which sift the divine.
In the dust today I eat without bread
And offer your name, again without wine
Towards the elements and coarse thunder,
The flutter of darts against heart and head.

(II)

Fergus placed you high above the altar;
The people below kneeling down for bread.
A numbness of fingers fumble the wafer
Whilst cowled above your arms are outspread
For us.
Your leaden face is smudged by blood
Thumb formed to uncommended beauty;
A touching in darkness as the mouth chews
And joints crack whilst obliged to another
A man returns to his place in the pew,
And today I have this your bread to offer.

(III)

You are the archer drawing the cord,
The amorous target tied to the tree,
Bound taught and open mouthed, still wailing
Across the sterile wastes of centuries.

A thin release, the wind stirs in caverns
And enters the ears as a sound of voices,
An absence of faith is ground for certainty;
In our heads there is no ground but noises,
A peal of bells, the laughter of children,
And Christus blow beaten on our dead sand sea.

Ikon of The Holy Spirit

Suddenly all around was nothing but light,
A chord of voices echoing with the void
Of light, resounding within and without,
A bright bell of light ringing with the Word.
And everything caught up into light
Where the Spirit is dumb and beyond herself,
Churning and boiling in an ocean of light
Till the smell of light snuffs out the senses,
And language falters without taking form.
Not as light perceived from within a shell
Opaque and distant to mere human hands,
But light transparent and vibrant and near.

As when thunder has cracked against the skull
And the heavens seeped in, as shafts of light
Transfigure a forest of broken trees
With the silent slow breathing of the Word
And the fierce uplifting rush of light.
So like the winds, yet blowing more constant,
As if a drone were sounded in the the stars
And groaned to the eternal weight of light,
History become the flicker of an eye
Before the piercing expanse of pure light
In the Word spoken and unutterable.

As though things translucent were torn apart,
Resung in the movement and grace of light
As canticles much brighter than the sun,
And yet one song in a symphony of light.
Wherein the comforter has stirred her wings
And her brooding face pressed on the waves,
Effervescent with the force and power of light,
The beyond that is always in our midst,
The eternal three dissolved into nothing,
A surrounding light caught up into light,
Storming the house of a quiet girl
With a branch of flame as the Word becomes flesh.

Ikon of The Son

What phlegm have the heavens spat on this man
That history's boots should clatter his language?
I would have listened by the underpass
Or from the metropolis above the Tyne,
Encountered the mystery's fists like a sage,
As one who would dance in the neon air,
And faced the electric bones of his face
With derisive fear for this assaulted king.
He is Lord indeed of our Mother church
But Mary where is your mothering of us all?
Speared he is squirming against the nails,
Ungracious, as one griped insane with pain,
Shouting in Hebrew to the Ecclesia,
Chanting in Latin by the Byker Wall.

Into My fingers

For Angela and her daughter

You came from the place where God incandescent
With darkness burned you in his ardour,
And I saw you come to me in the night
To tell me you were dead, your body burnt.

Yet your body was not ugly, nor skin palled.
And I cannot believe that you were taken,
I refuse it with the might of sticks and
Mountains, hurling fists of leaves against Him.

I, inopportune child, whilst you my mother
Kissed my soul. I was violent and brutal
To Him who loved you, who drew your
Hair, and curled you beside me, lovingly.

I wish for you with the curve of the shore
And ears bruised by shells that refuse to let
Me listen. I bleed with longing for you
My mum, waken to grasp the memory
Of your absence, beg gulls' beaks bruise
God to unhand you, into my fingers.

December 2001

Childhood

Your hands are dry in the cool wet grass
Your hair unkempt and face thin
I was your daughter, as sure as
 The sun's rays
Fork the soil

As sure as leaves like fish scales
Wrap your hollow body.
When the winds are blown back
     In their own mouths
And we have torn down trees like shreds
Of paper
     Then
   I shall be
Your daughter.

Frieze Farm

Under the apple tree with small fists of
Blossom, fat fingers tugging at your hair,
I gazed up to you through boughs and sunlight
As we walked towards the house and dad.

When the oil black crow died, crushed the window,
And I prodded his body with short sticks,
You stood so certain of his resurrection
Until the white earth picked his bones to bits.

You held me daily and my plump fists grew
Into angry hands of undue violence.
I have torn the flesh from the face of God
And known your motherhood as one of silence.

Under the apple tree the fine blossom
Dissipates with the wind and cherry breeze,
The woods beyond the farm, fine and splendid,
Are beyond the ken of present remembrance.

Aidan Unbound

Aidan stepped forward-
The arch of his back and beggar's ribs
Protruding beneath his thin rags.

He leans on the cross.
It is like an anchor,
Barbs rooted down in the flesh
Of the Earth, tugging.
Its mast high, cross arm taut.

He has his staff then
To cajole the people,
As a stern shepherd
To our delinquent laughter.

He has wrestled with Jacob
Up high on the fell tops,
He has watched the lambs
And cut his arms in winter
To bleed with us.

Christ be my platform,
My strong chevalier,
My mitre and robes,
My bread and vine.

He will wield that staff
And fracture the oceans-
Heading back up to Langholm
Beneath a crown of stars.

Oct 2007